Lonia:
A Conversion Story

James D. Greendyk

Reformation Heritage Books
Grand Rapids, Michigan 49525

Table of Contents

CHAPTER 1

A Praying Man

The winter night came quickly; the bitter wind howled through the trees, and the chill crept in under the door cracks and rusty windows of the small village home. Inside the house, a young girl huddled near a fire, trying to escape the cold night air. She was tired, and her belly growled with hunger, for she had not eaten a good meal all day.

The young girl was Lonia; she was twelve years old, and she lived in a small village in England with her mother and father. Lonia and her parents were very poor; her father made a little money as a coal miner, but he did not spend it wisely. He never brought home enough money to feed his hungry family. Day after day, her father came home angry, which caused Lonia and her mother many tears. As winter went on, the sadness turned to bitterness, and arguments filled their small home. "If only I had a loving mother and father like other children," thought

Lonia sorrowfully. But, it was not so, and poor Lonia hardly ever knew a happy time in her home.

Late one cold night, Lonia was lying in bed, when suddenly, she was jolted by a noise so loud that it shook her bed and rattled her windows. Lonia's heart jumped with fright. She tried to move, but she was frozen with fear. She heard the sound of footsteps outside, and suddenly a voice hollered, "Emergency! All men to the rescue!"

Lonia lay still in her bed and waited. Soon, the door to her room opened slowly, and Lonia's mother entered with another woman from the village. Her mother's eyes were filled with tears.

"Lonia," said her mother, weeping bitterly, "There's been a coal mine explosion, and Daddy has been hurt very badly."

"Oh, Mommy! Will daddy be alright?" asked Lonia fearfully.

"I don't know, my dear Lonia," her mother answered.

Lonia could not fall asleep for hours. As she finally dozed off, she could hear the two women talking in hushed voices. The neighbor woman exclaimed, "Oh, Rosa, how I wish our husbands could have different jobs. It's so terrible to live with the constant fear of explosions and accidents in the coal mines!"

The night dragged on, with no news at all about those hurt in the explosion. Finally, as the first rays of dawn shone through Lonia's window, she heard a knock on the door. Eager to hear news about her father, Lonia ran to the door and looked out; to her dismay, she was greeted by a policeman with a grim face. As soon as she saw his somber expression, she knew that her father had not survived. "Are you sure he's gone?" her mother cried desperately.

"Yes," answered the policeman sadly. "Every effort was made to save his life, but he died this morning. I'm so sorry."

The days following her father's death were lonely and difficult. Mother was distraught, and spent most days locked in her room, sobbing bitterly. Lonia had to find her own food, and was often hungry. She was grieving the loss of her father, and she felt forgotten and forsaken by her mother. Each night, Lonia cried herself to sleep, hungry and exhausted.

As the weeks passed, Lonia's mother fell terribly ill. Her condition worsened with each day, until one day, in the heart of winter, she died, leaving Lonia to fend for herself. As a poor orphan girl, Lonia was given servant's work. She had to work very hard only to earn her food. Her bed was a small pile of straw on the cold ground. No one in her new home seemed to care for her at all. Lonia felt lonely and unloved.

Months passed, and Lonia adjusted to her new job; she worked very hard to please the mistress of the house. One summer morning, Lonia was faithfully going about her chores when a man arrived at the gate. He seemed like a very kind man, but Lonia was shy, and dared not speak with him. The man had come for lodging, and would sleep in the room next to Lonia's. Late that night, after all her work was finished, Lonia lay quietly in her bed of straw, when to her surprise, she heard murmuring coming from the next room. Curious, Lonia put her ear to the wall, and heard the man speaking. He seemed to be talking to someone named God. Lonia heard the man mention her name. What was he saying? Lonia listened more closely, and heard the man say these words:

Lord, teach the dear little servant girl about sin. Teach her about Jesus Christ, the Savior of sinners, whose blood can wash away her sin. Lord, work all this in her by Thy Holy Spirit, so that she will be saved by grace, for Jesus' sake. Amen.

Children, do you thank the Lord for a mother and father who love you? Are you asking the Lord for the same thing the praying man asked for: to be taught about sin and to be saved by the blood of Jesus Christ through the work of the Holy Spirit?

CHAPTER 2

Fire

Lonia had never heard anyone speak to God before. As far back as she could remember, Lonia couldn't even recall hearing her mom and dad pray at all. She *did* remember them using the name of God when they were angry and shouting at each other. But the way this man was praying to God sounded very different from the angry shouts of her parents; it sounded tender and sincere. As she lay in her bed of straw, Lonia couldn't stop thinking about the man's prayer. "Why would he pray for me?" Lonia questioned quietly. "Why would he even care about me? No one else does." Suddenly, she burst into tears. Burying her head in the straw, she thought back on her mother and father, and an empty feeling filled her heart.

After some time, Lonia lifted her head and listened. Silence. The man was not praying anymore. "Is he sleeping?" Lonia thought to herself. "Has he left?" But, not many minutes passed before Lonia heard the man's voice once again; as she listened, she began to think about his words.

"What did he mean when he asked God to show me my sins? Who is the Lord Jesus Christ, and why would I need Him? Who is the Holy Spirit?" Lonia wondered. She was struck most of all when the man asked the Lord to help her to flee from the wrath to come—the wrath of an angry God and an eternity of hell. He prayed that she would find a hiding place in the bleeding wounds of the Lord Jesus by faith.

With all these thoughts going through her head, Lonia finally fell asleep. She slept soundly, hearing nothing, not even the scurrying mice or the screech owl that broke the night silence.

Suddenly, Lonia awoke with a start! For a moment, she forgot where she was. Then, she recognized the dreadful scent of smoke. The smoke began to burn her nose, and she squeezed her eyes shut. The night calm was broken abruptly by a frantic voice yelling, "Fire! Fire!" Lonia was terribly frightened, too scared to move. Crying, she screamed, "Save me! Save me! Someone please save me!"

Would anyone come to her rescue?

Lonia heard footsteps outside her room. A voice said loudly, "Stay where you are, child. I'm coming to get you." Lonia recognized the voice; it was the kind man who had been praying for her! Tears of relief flowed down her cheeks as she waited for him to come. It seemed like a long time before the door to her room swung open, and Lonia felt his strong, gentle arms pick her up and carry her away. Finally,

*Lonia felt his strong, gentle arms pick her up
and carry her away.*

they got outside, and Lonia could feel the cool night
air on her skin. Relieved to be free from the burning
smoke, she opened her tear-filled eyes. What a
horrible sight! The fire burned ferociously, devouring
the house. Amidst the roar of the fire, Lonia heard
the familiar voice again; the kind man was praying.

"Lord, save the souls of the poor people trapped

in this burning house! Save them from the wrath to come, for Jesus' sake. Amen!"

Still in the arms of this kind man, Lonia pressed herself close to him. His words rang in her ears, "Flee from the wrath to come!" Lonia couldn't forget these words, and she shuddered with fear.

Children, can you find these words in Matthew 3:7? What do you think they mean? Do you think God used these words to start His work of salvation in Lonia's heart? What about your heart?

CHAPTER 3

Survivors?

Flee from the wrath to come! These words kept running through Lonia's mind. What did they mean? Were they meant for her? Or were they only for the dying people trapped in the burning house? Finding it difficult to take her eyes off the fire, she kept seeing the shadows of people caught in the flames. She was terrified, but the kind man held Lonia securely. His strength comforted her; all the while, he continued to pray. His prayers impressed Lonia. She realized that he was a man that not only prayed in times of great need, as the fire raged about them, but also prayed in the quiet of his sleeping quarters, before the fire had ever begun.

The heat from the fire was great, so Lonia and the man stood at a distance, watching helplessly as the flames engulfed the house. Suddenly, over the roar of the fire, they heard loud voices shouting.

"Move back, move back!" yelled one fireman.

"Help! Help!" hollered another.

Lonia watched, terrified. The fireman was trapped under a falling wall! He struggled frantically, but could not break loose. Several other firemen came running to his rescue, pouring buckets of water to douse the fire that was quickly spreading. Finally, a few strong men were able to pull him loose, but his condition was not good.

Immediately, the praying man made his way to the firefighter. Kneeling at his side, he spoke kindly to the injured man. Lonia could feel his love and concern. The firefighter groaned in pain as the kind man offered a prayer for him, and he was quickly taken away to the hospital.

After several hours, the fierceness of the flames began to die down, and the darkness of night returned, but only for a short time. Soon, the first glimmers of dawn began to brighten the eastern skies; Lonia was exhausted and worried, wondering who had survived the tragic fire. She was deep in thought when a voice broke the morning silence.

"Did you live in this house? Is this your girl?" asked a large, stocky man standing in front of Lonia and her companion.

"No," replied the kind man politely, "I'm a traveler who lodged in this house for the night, and a short time after my evening devotions, I smelled smoke. As I ran to escape the flames, I heard the voice of this child crying for help."

Anxious to know more, the man asked about the other residents of the household. When he discovered that many had not been saved, he began to weep. "Oh, eternity, eternity!" he said mournfully, "how suddenly they found themselves in eternity!"

Lonia was left to ponder these somber words. Exhausted, Lonia and the man turned away from the scene of the fire, and began to walk down the long dirt road that led to the next town. It was a very long walk; with each step, the words she had heard echoed in her mind: *Eternity! Eternity! Flee from the wrath to come!*

Friend, do you pray to God only when you have troubles, or do you have a lifestyle of prayer? Lonia couldn't stop thinking about the word "eternity." What does this word mean to you? If you had to die today, do you know where you would spend eternity?

CHAPTER 4

Questions

Many hours passed before Lonia and the man saw another house. They walked on a dirt road along the edge of a dark forest. The wind blew fiercely, and Lonia's cheeks and fingertips stung with cold. She longed for the welcoming warmth of a crackling hearth, but she knew she was far from home. They walked in silence, with only the occasional sound of a morning birdsong. Lonia observed the forest as she walked. She was surprised by the life she saw around her, even in the early morning hours. Several deer were grazing on the frosty grass at the edge of the dirt road, and a squirrel scurried up a nearby tree. A chipmunk popped out from hiding to watch the travelers pass.

Every so often, Lonia heard the man humming a soft tune. She wanted to speak to him, but her shyness kept her silent. However, the man's gentle song eventually calmed Lonia's fear, and she found

"Sir, may I ask you a question?" Lonia said shyly.

the courage to speak just as the first beam of sunlight broke through the trees.

"Sir, may I ask you a question?" Lonia said shyly.

The man paused, surprised to hear Lonia speak, but quickly answered, "Yes, of course!"

Timidly, she shared her thoughts with the man. "I like the sound of the song you're humming. It makes me feel calm inside after such a terrible night. Can you tell me the name of the song? Are there any words?"

"Dear girl, this song is the prayer from Psalm 143. It is called 'Reliance and Supplication.' The words describe exactly what we are seeing this morning, and they tell how good it is to rest in the Lord."

Anxious to hear these comforting words, Lonia asked excitedly, "Please tell me!"

With a smile on his face, the man began to sing softly.

When morning lights the eastern skies,
O Lord Thy mercy show;
On Thee alone my hope relies;
Let me thy kindness know.
— Psalter 391:1

Lonia's heart was softened, and tears filled her eyes as she listened to the man's soothing voice. When he finished, she said quietly, "What a comforting song that is! It makes me believe that someone will care for me, and for you, too!"

They continued on the dirt path, and Lonia's shyness faded more with each step. The man was so kind, and she felt loved. Never in her life had she felt such security, or heard such beautiful prayers as this man offered. As the sun rose higher in the eastern sky, her hands and feet warmed, and the chill of the early morning faded; the morning sun seemed even to warm her heart, and she began to ask more questions.

"Sir!" Lonia said anxiously, "please tell me what the word *wrath* means. Last night, as I listened from my room, I heard you say to God that I needed to *flee from the wrath to come*. What did you mean? What does *eternity* mean? I have never heard these words before!"

Dear children, do you ever sing because you need the mercy of the Lord?

CHAPTER 5

Answers

The man began by asking a very important question. "What's your name, my dear?"

"Lonia," she answered softly.

"Well, it sure is nice to meet you. I certainly never thought I'd have a friend to walk with this morning. My name is Henry Doersluin, but you can call me Uncle Hank."

In answer to Lonia's questions, Uncle Hank began to tell a story. "Many years ago, Lonia, a boy broke into a bakery shop during the night and stole some bread. It wasn't long before the boy was caught by the police and taken away in the back of the police wagon. The little thief ended up spending the night in jail. The next morning, the police officer brought the boy back to the bakery. As they entered, the owner looked up in surprise. 'Well, good morning, officer!' he exclaimed cheerfully. 'Who do you have with you this morning?' The officer replied, 'I'm afraid this young fellow was caught stealing bread from your bakery last night. The mess you found in your bakery this morning was his doing. Before I take him down to the courthouse, I thought it would be good for you to meet him.' As the officer explained, the baker's face began to turn red, and his once cheerful voice was full of anger. 'Well, officer, how many scoundrels is this town going to put up with? If this were the first time I had been robbed, I might have more patience, but this is the third time, and I believe we need to be severe with this town troublemaker! This boy has broken the eighth commandment, "Thou shalt not steal," and God says that sin must be punished! The Bible speaks of God's wrath against sin; He punishes people for doing bad things!'"

Lonia interrupted the story, exclaiming, "Uncle Hank, I think I understand! Do you mean that this boy deserved to be punished for stealing from the bakery? Is that what wrath means?"

"Yes, Lonia. You see, when we do not obey the law that God has given us in the Bible, we are sinning. God is not pleased with us when we sin. He says that we will be punished when we sin. So, the word *wrath* means punishment from God for our sin," explained Hank.

"Oh, I understand now, Uncle Hank. When you prayed that I needed to flee from the wrath to come, you were praying for me because I have done bad things in my life. Is that what you call sin?"

"Yes, Lonia, that is exactly what I mean. God will punish all of the bad things that you and I have done in our lives. God knows every single time we sin. He hears when we speak, and He even knows what we're thinking. We can't hide anything from God! The Bible says, 'Be sure your sin will find you out.' Even if we sin in secret, God knows," said Uncle Hank.

"What did you mean, Uncle Hank, when you said I have to flee? Do I have to run away from this punishment?"

"Yes, Lonia," replied Hank. "If you do not find a way to escape, you will spend an eternity without God. Eternity is forever and ever; and being forever without God will be a terrible thing! But if our sin is forgiven through Jesus Christ, we will spend eternity with God, which will be the greatest joy imaginable!"

Lonia listened carefully, and tried to understand what Uncle Hank was telling her. They continued walking along the dirt path, talking excitedly, when suddenly, a loud rumbling noise startled them. They looked up, and were surprised to see a cloud of dust on the road before them as the rumbling noise came closer and closer!

Dear friend, in the story about the bakery, the town scoundrel was caught. Have you ever stolen? In Numbers 32:23, we read, "Be sure your sin will find you out." Do you believe that God knows each one of your sins? How do you think we can escape the wrath of God?

CHAPTER 6

An Unexpected Event

The rumbling grew louder; through the cloud of dust rising on the road, Uncle Hank and Lonia saw four men on horseback approaching, each with a sword in hand. Chills ran down Lonia's spine as she saw the threatening look in the eyes of the horsemen. As the horses slowed to a gallop, one of the men began to shout orders.

"Take that girl, tie her up and be off with her! As for you, Mr. Doersluin, what right did you have to take this girl with you? You will be charged with kidnapping!"

Uncle Hank looked alarmed, but answered the man with confidence. "Sir, she has no family to speak of. Her parents are dead, and the place where she worked as a servant girl was burned to the ground last night. She was left alone, with no one to care for her. What right do *you* have to treat her so roughly?"

With great boldness, Uncle Hank ordered Lonia's

A man on horseback approached with a sword in hand.

captors to release her. "Untie the girl immediately, or I will cry to God to send His judgment on all of you!"

The men sneered and laughed sarcastically. They advanced towards Uncle Hank, swords in hand. Suddenly, the first horseman swung his sword at Hank, barely missing his chest!

"Let that be a warning to you, Mr. Doersluin!" yelled another horseman gruffly.

Uncle Hank answered firmly, "Do what you must to me, but free the child. God sees, hears, and knows all that you do. 'Be not deceived; God is not mocked: for whatsoever a man soweth that shall he reap' (Gal. 6:7). 'God shall bring every work into judgment, with every secret thing, whether it be good, or whether it be evil' (Eccl. 12:14)."

To Lonia's shock, the captors dropped her to the ground and galloped away. Hank ran to her, untied her arms, and held her close. Lonia was overcome with fear and relief at the same time, and cried once more in the arms of the kind man.

"Oh, Uncle Hank," Lonia sobbed, "your God is so good! I thought my life was over!"

Uncle Hank spoke in a soft, but confident voice. "God is our refuge and strength, a very present help in trouble" (Ps. 46:1). Carrying Lonia to the edge of the dirt road, he set her on the soft grass, and began to pray. "Lord, Thou hast said in Thy word, 'Call upon me in the day of trouble: I will deliver thee, and thou shalt glorify me' (Ps. 50:15). Lord, we praise Thee and thank Thee for Thy great mercies, for Thou hast given immediate deliverance! Lord, remember us as we travel further and keep us under the shadow of Thy wings. Teach us how important it is for us to be ready to meet Thee, Lord, as we never know what a day will bring. Send someone, merciful God, to help us, for Jesus' sake. Amen."

Lonia waited to see if God would answer Uncle

Hank's prayer. Soon, some distance down the road, came the answer.

Friend, we never know what a day will bring. Death can steal us away without any warning at all. The Bible says, "Prepare to meet thy God" (Amos 4:12). We need to be ready to face God at any moment! How can we know that God is mighty to save us? Where does He promise to deliver us when we call on Him?

CHAPTER 7

Prayer Answered

Coming down the road was a beautiful, black, horse-drawn carriage. As Lonia watched the carriage approach, her mind was filled with questions. Who was in the carriage? Would they be kind? Perhaps they could give her and Uncle Hank a ride! The carriage drew closer, and rolled to a stop right in front of them.

The door opened, and a man with a long black beard, a top hat, and a black coat stepped out. Lonia suddenly felt frightened, remembering what had happened the last time they encountered someone on the road. She grasped Uncle Hank's hand tightly, but he assured her that they were safe. The man in the top hat approached, and reached out his hand to Uncle Hank. Uncle Hank shook his hand heartily, exclaiming, "Good morning, sir! Do you know how far it is to the next town? This girl and I have been walking for some time now, and are quite tired. Do you know where we can find a place to rest?"

"Well," responded the man, smiling, "God's ways certainly are amazing. Early this morning, as I was praying, I felt in my heart that someone needed help. However, I have been quite sick lately, so I thought it would be best to stay at home and rest. As I sat in my chair by the fireplace, reading my Bible, I read Galatians 6:9: 'Let us not be weary in well doing: for in due season we shall reap if we faint not.' Well, I was unable to sit in my chair any longer! I asked my servant to harness the horses and prepare the carriage. After about an hour, we rounded the last corner, and found you. Now I see why the Lord sent me out today!"

Lonia exclaimed, "Uncle Hank, this is the answer to your prayer! God heard you and sent this man to help us!"

The man with the top hat asked kindly, "Where are you headed?"

"It's been a long, troublesome night," answered Uncle Hank. "We were caught in a fire, and we were attacked by four horsemen, but the Lord has protected us the whole way. We are exhausted; would it be too much to ask you for a ride to the nearest town, sir? Do you know of a place to stay?"

Without hesitating, the man opened the carriage door, and welcomed them in. Lonia's eyes grew large with wonder as she climbed onto the soft cushion of the fancy carriage. How good it felt to rest her tired body! As the carriage rumbled down the road, Lonia looked out the window of the carriage, thinking of how amazing it was that God sent this man as an answer to Uncle Hank's prayer. Soon, Uncle Hank and the man got into a lively conversation; interested, Lonia began to listen to what Uncle Hank was saying.

"Sir, do you know the Lord?" Lonia heard him ask the man. "Have you ever felt the power and sweetness of His love? Has your sin ever become a burden to you? Are you washed in the blood of the Lamb?"

The man again smiled, and responded, "By the free and sovereign grace of God, I am a new man in Christ Jesus, a man I never would have been, had the Lord not struck my heart with Matthew 3:7, 'Flee from the wrath to come.'"

Lonia was surprised; she had heard those words before! Those were the same words Uncle Hank had said as they walked along the dirt road that morning!

Friend, are you able to answer yes to the questions that Uncle Hank asked the man in the carriage? Has God's Word ever made you realize that you are a sinner in need of a Savior?

CHAPTER 8

A New Discovery

Lonia was deep in thought as the carriage rumbled along. Once in a while, her thoughts were interrupted by Uncle Hank's conversation with the man. They were saying wonderful things about God that she had never heard before. She noticed the man had a book on his lap; he often leafed through its pages as he talked with Uncle Hank, and read some parts aloud. Lonia could see that the book was very precious to him, and she wondered what it was about.

Lonia watched in amazement as the man raised the book in the air, and said joyfully, "All that the Holy Spirit has taught me is found in this book! All I still need to learn must come from this book! I have found the greatest of treasures in this book; it taught me that I was a sinner (Rom. 3:23), and it taught me about Jesus Christ, the beloved Savior for such a lost sinner as I was (1 Tim. 1:15). What peace filled my heart when the Holy Spirit showed me that Jesus

Christ receives sinners (Luke 15:2). I was amazed that He could save a sinner like me!"

The man turned to Lonia, and said kindly, "If the Lord could save me, He can surely save you!" Lonia didn't know what to say. She felt that this book must be a great book, and that the person the man spoke about, Jesus Christ, was someone wonderful. As she listened to him speak, she could tell by the deep reverence and love in his voice that he loved his Savior.

The man turned again to Lonia. "Have you ever read the Bible?" he asked. "Do you know that the Bible is able to make you wise unto salvation, through faith in Christ Jesus?" (2 Tim. 3:15). Lonia answered timidly, "Well, Uncle Hank has told me of things in the Bible, but I've never read it myself."

The carriage rounded the last curve and pulled up to an iron gate. They drove up a long, narrow path until the carriage finally came to a stop. The door to the carriage was opened, and Lonia climbed out. Her eyes widened as she saw before her a beautiful mansion, lined with enormous trees. Immediately, Lonia's mind began to fill with questions. Who lived in this beautiful house? Were they going to stay here? Would she be a servant girl again? Would she sleep on a bed of straw?

Lonia was quiet, but she was anxious to find out what would happen. As she followed the man and Uncle Hank into the huge mansion, she was filled with excitement. They walked into the huge entryway, and Lonia was thrilled to see a fireplace with crackling flames. She walked over to warm her hands. Over the fireplace was a stone mantle, with words engraved on it. Lonia read the words to herself:

And if it seem evil unto you to serve the LORD,
choose you this day whom ye will serve;
but as for me and my house, we will serve the LORD.

These words made a deep impression on Lonia. She wondered how it could be evil to serve the Lord, when He is so good! If this was the same God that Uncle Hank and the man were talking about, there could be nothing evil about serving Him. She was lost in thought when Uncle Hank called her over with the good news that they had been invited to stay overnight with the man and his family. Lonia almost cried for joy at the thought of sleeping in a warm, comfortable bed. Soon, supper was served; it was a delicious, abundant meal. After they finished, the whole family gathered around the fireplace, and began to sing beautiful songs about God. Lonia watched and listened as the family sang together; their voices filled the room, and Lonia was overcome with happiness for one of the first times in her life. After they had finished singing, the father taught a lesson from his precious book, and the family prayed together, thanking God for His great mercies to them. They confessed their sins, and asked the Lord for forgiveness. Lonia listened carefully as the family asked God to keep them safe through another night, for Jesus' sake, and she had no doubt that the God who had been so good to her and Uncle Hank would surely answer the prayers of this wonderful family.

After they finished, the mother of the house led

She opened the Bible, and slowly began to read.

Lonia to the place where she would be staying. Lonia was delighted when she saw the cozy little bed, with blankets to keep her warm. Thanking the woman, she climbed up onto the bed. There, next to her pillow, was a book. Curious, Lonia picked it up; on the cover were the words, "Holy Bible." She opened to the first page, and there she found an inscription that read:

Dear Lonia,
This is God's gift to you. The Bible is able to make you wise unto salvation.
                              Love,
                              The Harmsons

Her very own Bible! Now she had a book just like the man did! Lonia was so thankful, and so excited to find the treasures that the man had been talking about all afternoon. She opened the Bible, and slowly began to read.

Dear friend, do you spend time reading your Bible every day? Do you realize what a treasure it is? Look up and learn 2 Timothy 3:14-17. What does Jesus say to you in John 5:39? What does Jesus mean when He says that the Scriptures contain eternal life?

CHAPTER 9

A Truthful Friend

Time passed swiftly, and Lonia read her new Bible late into the night. She was so excited about her treasure that she forgot her exhaustion; she read one story after another. One of the most beautiful stories she found was in a book called Luke. It was the story of a son who ran away from his family to live in the world, but later returned home to his father, poor, miserable, and needy; instead of turning him away, his father welcomed him home with open arms. Lonia was deeply touched by this story of forgiveness, and stored it away in her mind. But it was growing late, and her candle had grown dim. She finally closed her Bible, and put it safely in her bag for the next morning.

She was so thankful for her warm bed. No straw poked her back, no cold chilled her body, and no hard ground made her head ache. She felt safe, and what was better, she felt loved. Lonia fell asleep with a smile on her face, and slept soundly.

The sun shone brightly through her window and the birds chirped cheerfully as she awoke the next morning. She looked around, remembering with a joyful heart the stories she had read the night before. Suddenly, Lonia's thoughts were interrupted by the sound of voices downstairs, singing sweetly. How wonderful it sounded! Lonia lay very still, listening to the words.

> On the good and faithful, God has set His love;
> When they call He sends them blessings from above.
> Stand in awe and sin not; bid your heart be still;
> Through the silent watches, think upon His will.
>
> Lay upon God's altar, good and loving deeds,
> And in all things trust Him to supply your needs.
> Anxious and despairing, many walk in night;
> But to those that fear Him, God will send His light.
>
> — Psalter 7

Lonia scrambled out of bed, dressed quickly, and went downstairs, where she saw Uncle Hank and the family once again gathered around the fireplace. Uncle Hank was telling the story of all that had happened since he left his home two nights ago. He told how he had been on his way to a church meeting, but how God had other plans for him. Lonia was surprised to hear that, as he told the story, he did not sound disappointed or angry; on the contrary, Uncle Hank said that he understood the passage, "For my thoughts are not your thoughts, neither are your ways my ways, saith the LORD. For as the heavens are higher than the earth, so are my ways higher than your ways, and my thoughts than your thoughts" (Isa. 55:8-9). Uncle Hank thanked God for giving him the grace to accept his circumstances, and to Lonia's surprise, he especially thanked God for bringing Lonia into his life!

She listened intently as he continued to talk to the Harmson family, and she heard him saying, "I wonder what the Lord has in store for dear Lonia. It is my prayer that the Lord will teach her about sin, create in her a need for the Savior, and save her, so that she can live a truly Christian life."

The family soon finished their conversations, and each went about their daily work. Lonia met a daughter of the Harmsons, a girl named Priscilla, who was Lonia's age. They took to each other right away, and spent the day together, playing and laughing. Priscilla showed Lonia all around the house and through the gardens; she even took Lonia riding on the family's horses. As they rode along a quiet stream on the back of the property, they chatted and told each other stories. Lonia had many stories to tell, especially the story of her escape from the fire two nights before.

Priscilla listened attentively to Lonia's story. When she finished, Priscilla asked quietly, "Lonia, have you ever thought about dying?"

"Oh, Priscilla, I never did until that dreadful night of the fire. So many people died that night, and I thought for sure that I was going to die, too! I'll never forget the words I heard Uncle Hank pray to God just before the fire: he said I needed to *flee from the wrath to come!* Ever since then, I've thought so much about dying. Priscilla, I don't want to die yet. I'm so scared!"

"Well," asked Priscilla gently, "do you know why we have to die?"

"No," answered Lonia.

Priscilla began to explain, saying, "The Bible teaches us in Romans 6:23 that the wages of sin is death. That means that we have to die because we sinned. Also, God says in James 1:15 that sin, when it is finished, brings forth death."

Children, do you ever think about dying? Ask God to teach you the truth about sin and about death. We need to understand our sin so that we can understand our need for Jesus. If we know Jesus, we don't have to be scared to die at all!

CHAPTER 10

Death?

As they rode through the fields, the girls talked about God, the Bible, sin, and the Savior, Jesus Christ. Lonia shared with Priscilla about the emptiness she felt in her heart; she also told Priscilla the story she had read in her Bible about the runaway boy. She was so thankful for her new friend.

The sun was beginning to set, and the girls realized that they had been out all afternoon; darkness was setting in, and dinner would soon be ready. They turned their horses around and set out for the house, when suddenly, Lonia's horse was frightened by a loud noise in the woods. Spooked, the horse reared up on its hind legs; Lonia screamed and held the reins as tightly as she could. "Lonia, hold on!" Priscilla hollered, "I'm coming!"

"I'm trying!" screamed Lonia, but the horse bucked wildly again, and Lonia couldn't hold on any longer. She was thrown off, and fell to the ground a few feet away. The horse, still frightened, continued

*The horse, bucking wildly, threw her to the ground and
collapsed, right on top of Lonia's legs!*

to rear, and finally collapsed, right on top of Lonia's
legs! Priscilla watched the whole scene in terror;
when the horse collapsed, she ran to see if Lonia was
still alive. Lonia was lying face down, the horse
pinning her legs to the ground.

"Lonia, are you alive? Can you hear me? Lonia,
please answer me!" cried Priscilla frantically. But all
she heard was a faint moan. Priscilla realized that
she couldn't free Lonia; the weight of the horse was
too much for her to move. They were at the edge of
the property—that meant a twenty-minute ride to
the house! There was no time to waste, and she had
no choice but to go for help. Scared, but determined,
she mounted her horse and galloped towards the
house. As she rode, she prayed a fervent prayer:
"Lord, save Lonia! Please don't let her die. She isn't

saved yet; she's not ready to die! Please, Lord, have mercy on her."

Back home, dinner was cooking, and mother was looking anxiously out the window for the two girls as the night sky grew dark. She breathed a sigh of relief as she saw Priscilla come riding over the hill; however, her relief soon turned to fear as she realized that Priscilla was alone. She called out to her husband and Hank. The two men made their way immediately to the yard to meet Priscilla, who rode up, breathless and shaken. "Dad," she cried, "Lonia was thrown off the horse, and the horse is on top of her! She's pinned to the ground, and she won't answer me! I'm afraid she's really hurt!"

Her father's face grew grim. "Where is she, Priscilla?"

"She's at the edge of the property, way out by our summer camp!"

Her father took action. "Priscilla," he said, "go to the garage and tell James to harness the horses and get the carriage ready to go to the hospital." He turned to Hank. "Let's go!"

They ran to the stable, mounted the horses, and galloped towards where Lonia lay.

Dear friend, do you realize that your life can change in a moment's time? Every breath we breathe is a gift from God. Remember, the wages of sin is death, but the gift of God is eternal life (Rom. 6:23).

CHAPTER 11

Only a Thread

Hours later, the Harmson family was gathered in the waiting room of the hospital, anxious and tearful. Lonia was still unresponsive. All they could do was wait and pray.

Over the weeks, many God-fearing people came to visit Lonia. Though they did not know her, they knew and loved the Harmson family, and shared their concern. Many prayers were offered up for her; her most faithful visitor was Priscilla, who was at Lonia's side whenever she was free from school or chores. One evening, during a prayer meeting at the Harmson's church, an older member of the congregation was pleading with the Lord in prayer, when he was interrupted by a loud knock on the church door. He finished his prayer with one last plea for Lonia. At the door was a woman, another member of the congregation who had been visiting Lonia in the hospital that very evening. Her face was bright as she entered the church, bursting with good news for the praying people.

"Lonia awoke tonight! She spoke to me when I was with her at the hospital!" she said excitedly.

The congregation responded with praises and smiles. "Well," asked the minister anxiously, "what did she say?"

"Yes, that is the best part!" exclaimed the woman, "As she awoke, she looked up with pleading eyes, and said, 'I need to flee from the wrath to come! God, have mercy on me, please! I am a sinner!'"

How great was their joy! The congregation offered up prayers of thanksgiving for Lonia's physical and spiritual progress. Soon, several of them made their way to the hospital to see Lonia for themselves. When they arrived, Lonia was sitting upright in her bed; her eyes were open, but she was staring straight ahead. Priscilla drew close to the bed, and gently put her hand on Lonia's arm.

"Lonia," she whispered, "it's me, Priscilla." Lonia did not look at Priscilla, but tears filled her eyes. She said nothing, only closed her eyes and lay down quietly. Priscilla began to cry as the minister offered up a prayer to God. Priscilla's father, seeing her tears, took her in his arms and gently consoled her.

"My dear child, God hears our prayers. We must trust that He knows best. God tells us that the prayers of the righteous are not in vain. We must trust in this promise."

The members of the congregation made their way home, but Uncle Hank spent a sleepless night at Lonia's side. The doctor came in the next morning, and sadly informed Hank that Lonia might never be well again; the amount of brain damage seemed to be severe.

"I'm afraid that she is hanging on to life by a brittle thread," declared the doctor. "But with God, all things are possible. We must not be faithless, but believing. He is able to do exceeding abundantly above all that we ask or think!"

Hearing these words of faith, a calm came over Uncle Hank, and God granted him renewed strength and trust. He knew that God was always faithful to His Word, and he had faith that God would work all things for good. He spent the next few hours in fervent prayer, saying like Jacob, "I will not let thee go, except thou bless me!" (Gen. 32:26).

Dear friend, the words of the doctor were true for Lonia, but are also true for you and me. We hang on to life only by a thread. God has given us one precious soul. Jacob's prayer must be our prayer, too! We need the blessing of God's grace for our souls. Do not put off until tomorrow what must be settled today. Are you ready to meet the Lord?

CHAPTER 12

Good News

Over the next few days, visitors came and went, but to their discouragement, Lonia never uttered a word. Her eyes were closed and she lay motionless in her hospital bed. Even her nurses and doctors began to give up hope for her recovery, until late one night, a nurse heard some strange sounds coming from the end of the hall. Realizing that the sound was coming from Lonia's room, the nurse hurried to see if Lonia was all right. When she arrived, she was shocked to see Lonia sitting up in bed with her eyes open.

The nurse watched in amazement; Lonia was looking upward, clutching her Bible in her hands and exclaiming in a soft voice, "Lord, I must be saved! I cannot die as I am. I have too many sins! How will I escape Thy wrath? Lord, I know that my whole life is full of sin; even my heart is evil. I think wrong thoughts, and I say wrong words. I remember Uncle Hank asked Thee to teach me about the Savior, Jesus Christ, who can wash away sins with His blood.

Where can I find Jesus? Lord, please wash away my sins, and have mercy on me, for Jesus' sake."

Lonia lay down on her pillow, still holding her Bible close to her chest. Slowly, the nurse entered the room. Lonia looked to see who was coming. "Who are you?" she asked.

"I'm Mary, your nurse," replied the woman softly. "I am so glad to see that you are awake. How are you feeling, Lonia?"

"I'm Mary, your nurse," replied the woman softly.

"I'm not sure," Lonia said, "I don't feel well, but I am not even sure why I am here. Can you tell me where my friends are? What happened to me? Do you know Uncle Hank, and Priscilla? Where are they?"

"Slow down, Lonia," said Mary, smiling. "First of all, you're here because you hurt yourself falling off a horse. You've been unconscious for about two weeks. Your Uncle Hank and Priscilla have been here often; they've been sitting by your bedside, reading to you from the Bible, praying for you, and talking to you for the past few weeks. They are going to be so delighted to see that you're awake!"

Lonia nodded her head as she slowly began to remember what had happened to her at the Harmson's home. Everything began to come back to her: the afternoon ride with Priscilla, their talks about sin, about dying, and about Jesus, and then the horse that threw her off its back.

Her thoughts were interrupted by a shout down the hall. Lonia's nurse excused herself and left the room quickly. Lonia was too exhausted to keep her eyes open any longer, and she drifted off into a deep sleep.

She awoke the next morning feeling peaceful and refreshed. As she opened her eyes, she saw her nurse, Mary, preparing her medication. Lonia said good morning; remembering the frantic scene from the night before, she asked Mary, "Why did you have to rush out so suddenly last night? Why was everyone yelling?"

To Lonia's surprise, the nurse's eyes filled with

tears. "Lonia, last night a thirteen-year-old boy named Johnny died of leukemia."

Lonia's heart sank when she heard the sad report. "Do you know if he was ready to die?" she asked. "Was he ready to meet the Lord?"

"Well," said Mary, drying her tears, "I believe he was. Often I would walk into his room, and he would be praying, just like I heard you praying last night. He used to talk often about the precious blood of Jesus that washed away his sins. I remember him saying once that if the Lord Jesus hadn't loved him first, he never would have been saved. In fact, Lonia, just before he died, he sat up in his bed, with his arms stretched out as if he saw someone, and he said, 'Even so, come Lord Jesus!'" (Rev. 22:20).

Lonia was filled with joy. She imagined the boy stretching out his arms to Jesus as he was taken up into heaven. She smiled and exclaimed, "How happy Johnny must be, forever with the Lord!"

Dear children, we must see our sinfulness, and understand that only Jesus' blood can cleanse us from our sin. If we have been washed in His blood, when we die, He will say, "Come, ye blessed of my Father," and welcome us into heaven. If we are not washed in the blood of Jesus Christ, He will say to us, "Depart from me, ye cursed" (Matt. 25:34, 41). What will your end be? Repent of your sin, believe upon Jesus Christ, and be saved!

CHAPTER 13

A Hard or a Soft Heart?

Lonia spent a long time thinking about Johnny. Later that day, a new nurse came into Lonia's room to check on her. "Where's Mary?" asked Lonia curiously.

"Mary works at night, I work during the day," replied the new nurse curtly. Lonia could see she really didn't want to talk, but she decided to ask a question anyhow. "Did you know the boy that died last night?"

"Me? No, how would I know him? Anyhow, we have so many patients here that even if I had met him, I probably wouldn't remember him," the nurse grumbled.

Lonia was a bit taken aback, but she took a deep breath, and continued. "Well, the reason I'm asking is because I'd like to go to his funeral. Do you know when it will be?" Lonia waited for the response. The nurse looked annoyed.

"The funeral?" she repeated. "You want to go to the funeral?"

"I do," answered Lonia confidently.

"But you didn't even know the boy," snapped the nurse.

"No, I didn't, but he knew Jesus, and was ready to meet the Lord. I want to hear what the minister will say," explained Lonia.

"Well, that's crazy. You're too weak. You'll never make it to the church. You'd better just stop thinking about it right now, Lonia. Anyhow, I know the church where this boy was a member, and it's pretty strange. I've heard that the minister often talks about sin, and I don't think people really enjoy being told how bad they are." She frowned and continued, "If I were you, I'd stay as far away from that church as possible, or you may become just as strange as the people that go there. No minister is going to tell me how to live, or what I can and can't do." With that, the nurse turned and walked out of the room.

Lonia was left confused and saddened by the nurse's rude response. How could she talk about a minister like that? A minister is God's servant! Lonia was hurt, especially because she wouldn't be allowed to go to Johnny's funeral.

The hours passed, and Lonia spent the afternoon reading her Bible. As night fell, the door to her room opened, and Lonia was relieved to see Mary enter the room with a smile on her face. "Good evening, dear Lonia!" said Mary, but soon realized that Lonia's day had been anything but good. "Why, whatever is wrong?" she asked with concern. Lonia told Mary the whole story of the unkind nurse, and how much she wanted to go to Johnny's funeral.

Mary comforted Lonia and assured her that she

would ask the doctor and Uncle Hank what they thought about Lonia going to the funeral. "I can't promise you that they'll say yes, but I'll see what I can do," said Mary kindly. "In the meantime, why don't you look up Ecclesiastes 7:2, and tell me what it says."

Lonia reached for her Bible, looked up the verse, and read it aloud. "'It is better to go to the house of mourning than to go to the house of feasting: for that is the end of all men; and the living will lay it to heart.' Does that mean that God says it's good to go to a funeral?" she asked.

"Yes," replied Mary, "it does. Many people live for celebrations, but cannot bear the thought of going to church. Most people simply don't care about the ways of the Lord, Lonia. This is a very dangerous position to be in; God takes notice of such people, and watches them as they make themselves ready for hell, even when He calls and warns them to turn from their sin to Jesus. If they don't turn to Jesus, they will end up in hell."

Lonia shook her head sadly, thinking of the words of the unkind nurse earlier that day. She offered up a silent prayer for this nurse. "Dear Lord, help her to see Jesus! Help her to believe in Him!"

Lonia looked up with surprise as the door to her room opened, and Uncle Hank, Mr. Harmson, and Priscilla walked in. How glad she was to see their familiar faces! Uncle Hank walked over and hugged her, and Priscilla ran to the bedside and kissed her dear friend. They rejoiced to see Lonia awake, and told her how many people had visited and prayed for her. After a bit, their conversation turned to the story of the boy who had died.

"Did you know him, Uncle Hank?" asked Lonia.

"Well, no, I never met him," Uncle Hank explained, "but the Harmsons knew him. He went to their church. Priscilla said he was a boy who loved the Lord Jesus Christ. He suffered much, but now he is with our Father in heaven. Johnny was a child of the Lord, washed in the blood of the Lamb."

"Oh, what a wonderful thought!" exclaimed Lonia. "Forever with the Lord! No more tears, no more troubles, and no more sin! Forever holy, and forever rejoicing! I wonder if I will ever be ready to meet the Lord, like Johnny."

Dear friend, do you have a hard heart, or a soft heart? What is your attitude about church, about hearing God's Word preached, and about the minister? Look up Psalm 122:1. Are you glad to go to the house of the Lord?

Chapter 14

A Good Desire

Just as Uncle Hank, Mr. Harmson, and Priscilla were leaving the room to let Lonia rest, the doctor entered. He was a kind, compassionate man, who had shown much concern for Lonia's health.

"Hello, Lonia," he said in a cheerful voice. "How are you feeling tonight?"

"Quite well, thank you," replied Lonia.

"Do you have much pain in your legs?" he questioned, examining Lonia's legs as he spoke.

"Yes, I do, but I have an important question for you, doctor. Do you think I could go to Johnny's funeral tomorrow?" asked Lonia hopefully.

The doctor smiled, and said, "Ah, yes, Mary talked to me this afternoon about your request. As long as your friends help you, you should be able to go."

Tears filled Lonia's eyes. The doctor looked at her with surprise. "Why are you crying, Lonia? I thought you'd be happy with my answer!"

"Oh, doctor," exclaimed Lonia, "I am happy, but

ever since I heard about Johnny, and how he loved the Lord Jesus, I have prayed for the same faith that he had. I don't know if I'm ready to meet the Lord, like Johnny was. I know that I need to be saved from the wrath of God. I have been praying that God would make a way for me to go to Johnny's funeral, so that I could hear how I can be saved, too! I wonder if Jesus would save a sinner like me."

The room was quiet. After a few moments, Uncle Hank spoke up. "This man receiveth sinners, Lonia" (Luke 15:2).

"Who is the man that receives sinners, Uncle Hank?" asked Lonia.

"The Lord Jesus Christ receives sinners, Lonia. He tells sinners to come to Him. He promises that any sinner who comes to Him with all his or her sins will never be cast away. Jesus will never tell anyone that they've sinned too much to be forgiven by Him," explained Uncle Hank lovingly.

"Well, how do I come to Jesus? Where can I find Him?" Lonia asked anxiously.

"You can come to Jesus only by true faith, which is a gift from God, worked in the heart by the Holy Spirit."

"Uncle Hank, can you please tell me how that happens? I'm not sure I understand," said Lonia eagerly.

Uncle Hank responded with a smile, and said, "It all begins when the Holy Spirit teaches a person about sin, and how sin separates us from God, our Creator. This person begins to feel empty inside, because he understands how far he is from God, and has a true desire to be reunited with God. This desire prompts him to search for God in the Bible and at church. From God's Word, he learns about God's wrath against sin and about God's goodness in Jesus to sinners. These truths about God make him realize that there are so many ways in which he has sinned against God! He begins to confess his sins, both wrong thoughts and actions, and things he should have done, but didn't. He realizes that he truly deserves God's punishment for his sins."

"You see, Lonia," Uncle Hank continued, "we are

She closed her eyes, and exclaimed,
"Give me Jesus, or I will perish!"

supposed to love God above all, but ever since the Fall in Genesis 3, we love ourselves and hate God. So, we need to be rescued by the only perfect person, the very Son of God, Jesus Christ. When the Holy Spirit teaches us this, we realize that we can't do anything right, and that we need a perfect Savior. Then the Holy Spirit gives us grace to trust and believe in Jesus. Coming to Jesus with true faith means feeling our need of Him and surrendering all our sins and our entire life at His feet, believing that He is able and willing to save us by washing away our sins through His blood."

Lonia listened attentively. When Uncle Hank finished speaking, she closed her eyes, and exclaimed, "Give me Jesus, or I will perish!"

Friend, do you understand what it means to come to Jesus? Do you realize how much you need Him? You may come to Christ as a sinner, with all of your sins, sorrow, and guilt. Jesus is the Man of sorrows, but also the Man who saves! Behold the Lamb of God, which taketh away the sins of the world (John 1:29). He is willing and able to save you.

Chapter 15

A Solemn Sight

Lonia was so thankful that she could go to the funeral. That night after Uncle Hank, Mr. Harmson, and Priscilla left, Lonia lay in bed wondering what the minister would say. Unable to sleep, Lonia spent much time in prayer; the need of her soul was great. She thought about the words Uncle Hank had said, and about how much she wanted to be saved. She knew that she needed to be forgiven by Jesus, and prayed desperately for that forgiveness. "Lord, wilt Thou receive such a sinner as I am? Lord, help the minister to bring Thy Word tomorrow, and please, Lord, let me hear about Jesus, who can save me from my sin. Please, Lord, give me faith to believe in Jesus!"

The next morning, Lonia was ready to leave when Uncle Hank and the Harmsons arrived at the hospital.

"Good morning, Lonia! How are you feeling?" asked Mrs. Harmson.

"I feel quite well, thank you. I am looking forward

to hearing the minister talk about Jesus today," Lonia answered with a smile.

The trip to the funeral was long and quite difficult for Lonia. The bumpy roads jolted her weak legs; she often winced in pain. As they neared the church, Lonia could hear music coming from inside; it was a slow, sad melody.

"Mrs. Harmson, do you know the words to this song?" she asked as they approached the church entrance.

"Yes, Lonia, I do. The words are based on Psalm 51." She began to sing along softly with the music:

> *God be merciful to me,*
> *   On Thy grace I rest my plea;*
> *Plenteous in compassion Thou,*
> *   Blot out my transgressions now;*
> *Wash me, make me pure within;*
> *   Cleanse, O cleanse me from my sin.*
>
> *My transgressions I confess,*
> *   Grief and guilt my soul oppress;*
> *I have sinned against Thy grace*
> *   And provoked Thee to Thy face;*
> *I confess Thy judgment just,*
> *   Speechless, I thy mercy trust.*
>
> *I am evil, born in sin;*
> *   Thou desirest truth within.*
> *Thou alone my Savior art,*
> *   Teach Thy wisdom to my heart;*
> *Make me pure, Thy grace bestow,*
> *   Wash me whiter than the snow.*
>
> *Broken, humbled to the dust*
> *   By Thy wrath and judgment just,*

Let my contrite heart rejoice
 And in gladness hear Thy voice;
From my sins O hide Thy face,
 Blot them out in boundless grace.

—Psalter 140

"Oh, Mrs. Harmson, what beautiful words!" Lonia said joyfully. "They describe what I feel in my heart, and what I've told the Lord. I truly want to be delivered from my sins today! Maybe the minister will tell me how Jesus can save me from all my sins."

The church was full; people overflowed out into the street. Long lines extended out the church doors and around the corner. All was silent, except for a horse-drawn carriage that was approaching slowly up the street. Lonia saw a group of people walking very slowly with their heads bowed. Suddenly she realized what was happening; this was the carriage carrying Johnny's coffin, and following, was his family. Lonia's eyes were fixed on the small coffin; never before had she seen such a solemn sight. She felt that death was serious and final. Johnny's life on earth was over, but he had an eternity to live! As she watched the somber scene, some words echoed in Lonia's mind: "For the wages of sin is death; but the gift of God is eternal life through Jesus Christ our Lord" (Rom. 6:23).

Dear child, you must be ready for death before it comes. Life is so short; we will all die one day, and eternity is forever! If you die today, will you spend eternity in heaven or in hell?

Chapter 16

Hope!

The black carriage came to a halt in front of the church. Many people were weeping as the men took Johnny's coffin down and carried it into the church. They were all pained by his death; they had prayed so much for the Lord to spare his life. They were learning the painful lesson of submission to the will of God. God was showing them that when death comes, "There is no man that hath power over the spirit to retain the spirit; neither hath he power in the day of death: and there is no discharge in that war, neither shall wickedness deliver those who are given to it" (Eccl. 8:11).

Uncle Hank carried Lonia to a place where she could sit down, near the front of the church. The minister began by asking the congregation to sing Psalter 140; he explained tenderly that this had been Johnny's favorite song, and that he often sang it during the days before he died. He told how Johnny had learned this song as a little boy, but that God had made it precious to him when he was nine years old. Johnny could not thank God enough for Jesus Christ, who bought this mercy for him on the cross.

As Lonia listened to the minister tell the story of how Johnny came to believe in the Lord Jesus, she was filled with joy and longing. She thought of how she too needed God's mercy. Now, in God's house, she was hearing of someone who had needed God's mercy, asked for it, and had received it! If only the same could be true for her! "Oh, Lord," she prayed, "there was mercy for Johnny, is there mercy for me too? Lord, please, have mercy on me; I am such a sinner. Save me too, Lord!"

The beautiful words of the song comforted Lonia. The minister read from Luke 15:1-10, about Jesus Christ, who receives sinners and eats with them. He read the story of the good shepherd who went out to look for his lost sheep, and did not return home until it was safely with him. What a beautiful message! The minister pleaded in his prayer that God's people would find comfort in Christ Jesus and that the unsaved would seek after Jesus. As he prayed to God, he pleaded for those who were living wicked lives, on the edge of hell itself; Johnny's death was a somber warning to all that life is short and fleeting, and that now is the day of salvation. He prayed for all the young children who had lost their godly friend. Finally, he prayed for the boys and girls who were crying out for God's mercy. "Dear Lord," he prayed, "may they see that Jesus Christ receives all kinds of sinners! Bring the message of salvation through Jesus Christ to their troubled souls. May they rejoice in

Jesus, through the work of the Holy Spirit. May sinners be saved today, and may they find true happiness in Thee, for the sake of Jesus Christ. Amen!"

As tears streamed down her face, Lonia closed her eyes and offered up a silent prayer, saying, "Lord, could it be that my prayers are being answered? Oh, Lord, save me, and help me to find true happiness in Thee!"

How wonderful is God's way of bringing a sinner to Himself! He drew Lonia closer and closer, helping her to understand her sin, and how she desperately needed a Savior to redeem her. Her heart resounded with the words of the song and the minister's prayer, for she felt the same need within her own soul. She listened with an open heart as the minister began his message.

"Dear parents, brothers, sisters, family, friends, boys and girls, even in the midst of your great grief today, the Lord comforts you, saying, 'Blessed are the dead which die in the Lord from henceforth: Yea, saith the Spirit, that they may rest from their labors; and their works do follow them' (Rev. 14:13)."

Dear friend, when you die, will your parents and family rejoice and praise God whose mercy in Jesus Christ saved you from your sins? Are you a child of God, or are you still lost in your sin?

Chapter 17

Welcome, Sinner!

What a beautiful message God gave the minister to deliver! He spoke words of comfort to Johnny's family, and directed them to turn to Luke 15:2, "This man receiveth sinners." Lonia's heart warmed at the idea that *this man* would befriend poor, wretched sinners. Was *this man* the Savior Jesus Christ that Uncle Hank had told her about? Suddenly, she began to understand the beauty of the words, "This man receiveth sinners." How sweet, how loving, and how powerful this Savior must be!

The minister continued, telling the story of the people who accused Jesus of eating with sinners. Lonia listened eagerly to his message. He spoke of the Savior, saying,

Dear friends, this verse has been held dear by children of God throughout history. But who originally spoke these words? They were not uttered by admirers of Jesus, but by His enemies! We read that when "all the publicans and sinners drew near to hear him, the Pharisees and scribes murmured, saying, 'This man receiveth sinners, and eateth with them.' These words came as spiteful criticism from the lips of ignorant Jewish leaders who simply could not understand how Jesus could associate with the lowest of society. These words were meant for evil, but God used them for good! These bitter words, which were meant for scorn and reproach, have been used by God to draw sinners to Jesus. The very act the Pharisees scorned was that which Jesus came on earth to accomplish! Just like the good shepherd, Jesus' mission was to find and rescue His lost sheep. Little did the Pharisees and scribes realize the precious truth of the words they had spoken.

Dear friends, the Lord Jesus is the only one who can receive sinners! He opens His arms to children, adults, parents, and grandparents; Jesus draws them to Himself and receives them, pardons them, makes them holy, and prepares them for an eternity in heaven. Do not fear that you are too sinful, too old, or too young; Jesus receives all types of sinners; no one is beyond His reach! Jesus did not come to save good people, but to bring guilty sinners to repentance and salvation. He is still the Savior today; He is still the Friend of sinners!

Johnny knew this Savior, Jesus Christ. And what about you? Do you understand that you are sinful, and that you desperately need the Lord Jesus to save you from your past, as well as a lifetime of continual sin? Well, dear friends, I beg you, do not wait any longer! Make haste! Jesus is ready, able, and willing to receive you. The promise is in His Word, "This man receiveth sinners." He lived a perfect, blameless life so that He could save wretched sinners. He suffered and died on the cross, and shed His precious blood for such sinners. Now He calls you, and you may come to Him, no matter how old or young you are.

Friend, you need this Savior! Come to Him, just as you are; though your sins weigh you down, though you are compassed on every side by fears and guilt, Jesus will receive you graciously, He will pardon you fully, and He will give you eternal life. He gives us this firm promise in His Word, when He declares, "All that the Father giveth me shall come to me; and him that cometh to me, I will in no wise cast out."

He is calling you! "Come unto me," He cries, "all ye that labor and are heavy laden, and I will give you rest" (Matt. 11:28). Do you hear Him, dear friends? Do you believe Him? Be assured, "this man receiveth sinners." Do not go lost because you refuse to come to Jesus to be saved!

Lonia was overcome by joy and gratitude. Here was the answer to her prayers! As the minister ended in prayer, she begged, "Lord Jesus, please receive me, a poor sinner!"

Dear reader, only Jesus can save poor sinners. Have you come to Him for salvation?

Chapter 18

Attacked

Slowly, the church emptied; people filed out silently. They were grieving deeply, but many were comforted by the words of hope they had heard. Uncle Hank carried Lonia out of the church. She was still thinking of the words the minister had spoken about: "This man receiveth sinners." How precious these words were to her!

Lonia watched as the coffin was carried out of the church; she thought of Johnny, rejoicing in heaven. Suddenly, her thoughts clouded over; it was as if someone was whispering slyly in her ear, "And what about you? Do you really think that Jesus will save you? You've never even gone to church! All of these feelings you're having for Jesus are just imaginary; besides, you're too young! You need to live a little, to have some fun before you get into all this serious religion. Wait until you're older to become a Christian. You don't have to worry about death now; true, Johnny died, but he had a disease."

Suddenly, her thoughts clouded over;
it was as if someone was whispering slyly in her ear...

Lonia was confused and frightened. Why was she thinking such strange things? Why now, after the Lord Jesus had become so precious to her? She became angry with herself, questioning, "Lord, why am I thinking these things? I'm so sorry! I don't understand why my heart is thinking like this, especially after I've just begun to love the Lord Jesus. Make these thoughts go away, Lord!"

Meanwhile, the crowd of people continued walking towards the cemetery; Lonia was carried to a place next to the open grave. As she looked down into the deep hole, she shivered. She had never seen an open grave before; horrible thoughts attacked her as she stared down into the darkness. Soon, the minister's voice awakened her; he was reading some very solemn words about the last judgment, when the wicked would be cast into hell, and the righteous would be taken into heaven. He spoke joyfully about the righteous who die in the Lord's arms; they would be forever with the Lord! They would never again experience pain, suffering, or dying, because eternal life was God's free gift to them. They would forever rejoice with the Father, the Son, and the Holy Ghost.

Suddenly, the minister spoke some words that seemed to be directed right at Lonia. She listened carefully as he spoke: "If there are boys, girls, parents or grandparents here who have seen the beauty of the Savior, but are being attacked by troubling thoughts, I want you to know that this attack comes from Satan, the father of lies. He works hard to keep poor sinners from Jesus. But be of good cheer, for all power is given to Jesus in heaven and on earth. Jesus will prevail, because He has conquered the devil on the cross by His resurrection from the dead. Jesus lives at the right hand of His Father to care for and deliver needy sinners from their sin and from Satan. If you are being attacked, pray to the Father for deliverance. God says to you, 'Fear not, I will help thee. I will deliver thee. I will save thee.' Jesus promises in Luke 19:10, 'For the Son of man is come to seek and to save that which was lost.' Jesus faced all of the attacks of Satan in the desert, and He defeated the devil, for your sake (Matt. 4). God declares, 'Call upon me in the day of trouble: I will deliver thee, and thou shalt glorify me' (Ps. 50:15). 'For we have not an high priest (Jesus) which cannot be touched with the feelings of our infirmities; but was in all points tempted like as we are, yet without sin. Let us therefore come boldly unto the throne of grace, that we may obtain mercy and find grace to help in time of need' (Heb. 4:15-16)."

Lonia was so thankful for these words of promise and encouragement! Immediately, the troubling thoughts disappeared from her mind, and her desire for Jesus became even stronger. As the minister finished his prayer, the crowd began to disperse. Lonia remained at the gravesite, watching as Johnny's body was laid in its final resting place. Uncle Hank stood quietly at her side until she was ready to leave, and he carried her gently to the carriage. Sensing that she was still deep in thought, he said to her in a kind voice, "'Blessed are they which do hunger and thirst after righteousness: for they shall be filled' (Matt. 5:6). Lonia, I am praying for you."

"Thank you!" said Lonia, with humility and thankfulness.

Children, Jesus saves! The devil is a liar! Have faith in Jesus Christ; He will deliver you from all evil.

Chapter 19

Need We Be Angry?

Lonia found it very difficult to return to her lonely hospital room. She had so cherished the fellowship with believers; the thought of being alone again made her gloomy. She grumbled to herself as the carriage pulled up in front of the hospital; when Uncle Hank picked her up to carry her inside, she began to cry.

"Mrs. Harmson, do I have to go back to the hospital? Why can't I go home with you?" she asked tearfully.

"Oh, Lonia, dear, you're too weak, and your leg injuries require more help than we can give you at home," answered Mrs. Harmson.

Lonia's tears quickly turned to bitterness, and she became angry. As her friends settled her back into her hospital bed, they could see that Lonia was unhappy. Quietly, but firmly, Uncle Hank put his hand on her shoulder, and quoted Ephesians 4:26-27, "Be ye angry, and sin not: let not the sun go down upon your wrath: neither give place to the devil." Uncle Hank explained kindly to Lonia, saying, "God uses difficult times in our lives to teach us patience and submission. The devil tries to stir up our hearts and minds to think evil thoughts about God, and to be angry about our situation in life. He wants us to think that God is cruel and unkind. But God has a purpose in every affliction and trial; He allows us to go through trials to show us more of our sin and rebellion so that we will cry to Him for grace and help.

"Lonia," Uncle Hank continued, "God works in mysterious ways to teach us how sinful our hearts are. He wants us to learn to cast all of our burdens on Him, and beg Jesus Christ for deliverance from sin. God teaches us that Jesus is the Man of Sorrows, and that He is acquainted with our griefs. Despite all our sin and rebellion, Jesus receives sinners, for He is the Friend of sinners! It is His grace we need, Lonia."

After making sure that she was settled into her room, Uncle Hank and the Harmson family left Lonia for the night. Alone, Lonia was able to think long and hard about the instruction Uncle Hank had given her. His words convicted her, and she confessed her sin to God, just as Uncle Hank had instructed. She cried, "God be merciful to me, a sinner! I cannot bear these troubles alone!"

Lonia opened her Bible, and turned to the Psalms, where she had often found comforting words. In Psalm 30:5, she read, "Weeping may endure for a night, but joy cometh in the morning." What a promise! Lonia asked the Lord for this joy; she was certain that He would once again answer her prayer, and she fell asleep in peace.

Dear friend, Jesus alone is fit to meet your needs! Are you turning to Him, and trusting that He will not cast you away because of His amazing grace?

Chapter 20

A God-sent Friend

Lonia awoke early the next morning to the clatter of hospital noises outside her door. As she stretched and rubbed her eyes, she heard the sound of a voice coming from down the hallway. It was a woman's voice, singing sweetly:

> *I must tell Jesus all of my trials;*
> *I cannot bear these burdens alone:*
> *In my distress He kindly will help me,*
> *He ever loves and cares for His own.*
>
> *I must tell Jesus all of my troubles;*
> *He is a kind, compassionate Friend:*
> *If I but ask Him, He will deliver,*
> *Make of my troubles quickly an end.*
>
> *I must tell Jesus! I must tell Jesus!*
> *I cannot bear these burdens alone;*
> *I must tell Jesus! I must tell Jesus!*
> *Jesus can help me, Jesus alone!*

Lonia's heart began to beat faster. She would love to talk with this woman! But she was so shy—how would she ever build up the courage to go visit a stranger? As she thought about what to do, the words of Psalm 30 came back to her. It seemed as if God was saying, "Lonia, when you were grieving over your sin, didn't you ask Me for joy? Well, I am providing an answer to that prayer! Don't be afraid to go talk with the woman."

With newfound determination, Lonia climbed down from the hospital bed into her small wheelchair. She had never been in the wheelchair without her nurse; nervously, she wheeled her chair all the way down the long hallway until she reached the

*She took a deep breath, and raised
her fist to knock on the door.*

woman's room. She took a deep breath, and raised her fist to knock on the door. At that very moment, a guard rounded the corner, and looked in surprise at Lonia.

"What are you doing here by yourself?" asked the man anxiously.

Lonia was scared; she couldn't think of anything to say.

When Lonia didn't answer, he asked, "Where is your room?"

Lonia pointed timidly in the direction of her room. The guard walked briskly to the desk and whispered something to the nurses. Lonia saw him pointing at her; the nurse left quickly, and returned with a doctor who looked very concerned.

"Lonia!" exclaimed the doctor. "What are you doing out here alone with two broken legs? How did you get here?"

Lonia was terrified. She couldn't work up the courage to tell the doctor why she had wheeled herself down the hallway; they would surely be upset with her! In the midst of the commotion, a woman appeared in the doorway of the room. She was old, wrinkly, and hunched over, barely able to walk. As she surveyed the situation, she spoke in a kind, soft voice.

"What's going on?" she queried. "Is there something wrong?"

"Why, yes," answered the doctor. "We found this girl all alone outside of your room!"

"Really? Let me have a look at her," said the old woman, shuffling closer, to get a better look at Lonia. "Why, yes, I know this little girl. Lonia, isn't it? Yes, didn't I see you at Johnny's funeral yesterday?" she asked knowingly.

"Yes, ma'm," Lonia answered quietly.

Frustrated, the guard interrupted the conversation.

"Excuse me, ma'm, but I believe it is time for you to return to your room, and this girl to hers. If you want to talk later, feel free to do so, but right now, we have other matters to tend to."

To her dismay, Lonia was returned to her room and put back into her bed. Her mission had failed; however, her courage was restored. She was surprised that the woman remembered her from Johnny's funeral! She was even more excited to talk with this woman.

Night fell, and once again, nurse Mary came in to check on Lonia.

"Hello, dear. The day nurses told me about your little adventure early this morning. They said they found you alone in Mrs. Kaplan's doorway this morning. Lonia, if you wanted to meet her, you should have asked me. She's a very nice, wise old woman, just like a loving grandmother. I think you'll find her to be wonderful. She reads her Bible all the time. In fact, she is a member of the same church that Johnny attended."

Lonia was thrilled. "She must love the Lord Jesus," she said. "The song she was singing was so beautiful! That's what drew me to her room."

"Well," said Mary, "you'll be happy to know that she's asked to see you. I'll take you to her room first thing tomorrow morning."

A smile spread across Lonia's face as she thought to herself, "God is so good. Just as He promised, joy comes in the morning!"

Children, do you ever try to talk to your friends about Jesus? Do you know the joy of having a friend you can talk to about Jesus?

Chapter 21

Lessons from Grandma

Lonia spent hours with Mrs. Kaplan. She was just like a loving grandmother, and Lonia's shyness melted away completely.

"I saw you at Johnny's funeral yesterday, Lonia," remarked Mrs. Kaplan. "Did you hear the minister's message about Jesus receiving sinners? Do you know what that means, Lonia?"

"Yes, I heard the message," replied Lonia enthusiastically. "Uncle Hank explained to me how Jesus receives sinners. But I am still wondering if Jesus could really receive me."

"Lonia, do you feel that you are a sinner?" asked the kind old woman.

"Yes, oh yes, and I wish with all my heart that I had never sinned against God. Even yesterday, when I returned to the hospital, my attitude was so sinful!" She explained to Grandma Kaplan how angry she had been about returning to the cold, lonely hospital. She shared how Uncle Hank had been so kind, yet firm, in telling her that she was sinning against God in her anger (Eph. 4:26). Soon, Lonia found herself telling Grandma all about her past: how her parents had died, how she had become a servant girl, and how she had to sleep on a hard bed of straw. With a smile, she told Grandma how she had heard Uncle Hank's prayer through the thin wall in the servant's quarters; and finally, she told with excitement how Uncle Hank had rescued her from the burning house.

As Lonia told story after story, the old woman listened intently, nodding and smiling. She could tell that Lonia was a poor, needy sinner, who clearly understood her need of the Lord Jesus, but still had much to learn. Lonia was glad to tell Grandma all about herself; it made her feel like Grandma had known her for a long time.

"What about you, Grandma?" she asked with a smile. "Tell me some stories about your life. When did you first find out that you were a sinner in need of Jesus?"

And so, Mrs. Kaplan began to tell the story of how the Lord had found her, taught her about sin and gave her faith to believe in Jesus. She expressed her joy in living for God and serving Him. Lonia listened very carefully as Mrs. Kaplan talked to her about Jesus' willingness to save sinners.

"Oh, dear Lonia," she exclaimed sweetly, "do you realize that Jesus is even more willing to save you than you are willing to be saved? He has come to seek and to save that which was lost (Luke 19:10). How wonderful it is that the Father has laid help upon One that is Mighty (Ps. 89:19). Jesus is able to save

Mrs. Kaplan talked lovingly of the good news of salvation.

to the uttermost all those that come to God through Him, and that he ever lives to make intercession for sinners" (Heb. 7:25). Mrs. Kaplan talked lovingly of the good news of salvation, and Lonia felt an irresistible desire in her heart for Jesus and His loveliness.

Grandma and Lonia were very thankful for each other's company. They ate lunch together, all the while speaking of God and His grace. After they finished lunch, Grandma said, "Lonia, hand me my Bible, please. It's over there, on my night table. I want to share something with you, my dear."

Adjusting her glasses, Grandma began to read from Isaiah 40. When she finished, she lowered her Bible and said to Lonia, "My dear Lonia, do you hear what God is telling us? He says, 'There is no God beside me; a just God and a Savior.... Look unto me, and be ye saved, all the ends of the earth: for I am God, and there is none else.' Aren't these beautiful words, Lonia? Our God is a God of truth; what He speaks will happen. People from every nation will be saved and will worship the Lord. They will cry joyfully, 'In the Lord, I have righteousness!' That means that we are made right with God through Jesus, who was the perfect God and man (1 Cor. 1:30).

"Lonia," she continued, "Jesus is the strength of His people. He helps us carry every burden we have throughout our life. Now you can understand why I sang the song that said, 'I cannot bear my burdens alone.' I can not overcome any difficulty without the strength of Jesus, or do anything pleasing to God. I can not even bear weakness, nor can you accept your stay in the hospital without the grace of Jesus. Lonia, Jesus draws people to Himself. Listen to what the Lord says, 'Even to him shall men come' (Isa. 40:24). O blessed Savior! Redeemer! Strength! Jesus receives sinners! Don't turn to any other savior or redeemer. If we want to draw near to God, we must be washed in the blood of Jesus Christ. He invites us, Lonia; He calls us, saying, 'Come unto me, all ye that labour and are heavy laden, and I will give you rest' (Matt. 11:28)."

Friend, have you felt your need of Jesus, and believed the good news about Him? He will give you rest!

Chapter 22

The Price for Sin

Days passed by, and Lonia's prayers became more fervent. She begged God to show her His mercy. However, through all her reading and prayers, Lonia was bothered by one question. She had read in Isaiah 42 that God is "a just God and a Savior." Late one evening, Lonia was reading Exodus 34, and two verses caught her attention. "The LORD, the LORD God, merciful and gracious, longsuffering, and abundant in goodness and truth. Keeping mercy for thousands, forgiving iniquity and transgression, and that will by no means clear the guilty" (vv. 6-7). What was God saying about Himself? Lonia couldn't see how God could be full of mercy for sinners, but not willing to clear those who are guilty. As she thought, she prayed that God would help her understand what He was saying. She made her way to Mrs. Kaplan's room, and knocked softly on the door.

"Come in," called Grandma. Seeing Lonia, her

face lit up with a smile. "Well, Lonia, how are you this morning?"

"Grandma, I'm a bit confused, and I was hoping you could help me," replied Lonia.

"Well, I'll certainly try," answered Grandma cheerfully. "What's bothering you, dear?"

Lonia took a deep breath, and began to explain her confusion. Grandma listened attentively to Lonia's questions. Thinking for a moment, she reached for her Bible, and explained: "You see, Lonia, God is just, or perfectly righteous in every way. We are sinners, who live entirely unjust lives. We cannot do anything right; we can never please God on our own. But because God is perfectly holy, He cannot let our sins go unpunished. That is why God says in Exodus that He will not clear the guilty. So, unless we repent of our sins and flee to Jesus to be our substitute, we will eternally pay for the sins we have committed. Lonia, hope in the LORD: for with the LORD there is mercy, and with him is plenteous redemption. And he shall redeem Israel from all his iniquities (Ps. 130:7-8). The beautiful truth is that God has given His Son to be our substitute, and if we turn to Him, He will save us from our sins!"

"Grandma," questioned Lonia, "what does it mean to repent of our sin and flee to Jesus?"

Grandma paused for a moment, then continued thoughtfully, "The Holy Spirit shows us how wicked our hearts are. When we begin to understand how much we've offended God, we feel sorry, confess our sins to God, and trust in Jesus for forgiveness. Does that make it any clearer?"

"Yes, I see. But Grandma, how can Jesus pay for our sins?" Lonia asked.

Grandma replied with confidence, "When He died on the cross, He paid for all the sins of those who believe in Him. He willingly gave Himself to be nailed to the cross for the sake of sinners. While He was dying on the cross, His blood ran from the wounds in His hands, feet, and side. This blood is the precious price that Jesus paid to save sinners. All the sins for which you and I, dear Lonia, deserve to be eternally punished, Jesus paid for with His own blood. Because Jesus has paid this price, God the Father can say, 'Deliver him (a sinner) from going down into the pit: I have found a ransom' (Job 33:24). Lonia, when Jesus died on the cross for His people, He was saying that He loves His people so much that instead of seeing them punished forever, He would give His own life in their place. God says, 'But God commendeth His love toward us, in that, while we were yet sinners, Christ died for us. Much more then, being now justified by his blood, we shall be saved from wrath through [Jesus]' (Rom. 5:8-9)."

"Oh, Grandma," Lonia asked excitedly, "Could Jesus have died for a sinner like *me,* too?"

"Yes, Lonia," Grandma replied confidently, "for you, too."

Children, there is a fountain of blood which washes away even the worst sins of the worst sinner! Will you come and be washed in this fountain?

Chapter 23

Lessons in Faith

"Grandma," said Lonia, "I can hardly believe that Jesus could have carried all my sins to the cross, and paid for my sins with His blood!"

Grandma answered with love, "Oh, Lonia, not believing that Jesus has carried your sins to Calvary's cross is called unbelief! Unbelief is the worst of all sins; it means that you do not believe Jesus when He tells us that He has died for lost sinners. God knows that many people struggle with this sin; that's why when Jesus showed Thomas His pierced hands and side, He said to Thomas, 'Be not faithless, but believing' (John 20:27). Jesus tells us that we must believe that He came to save sinners who cannot save themselves. He obeyed God's commandments perfectly. He gave up His very life as a sacrifice, and just before He died, He cried from the cross, 'It is finished' (John 19:30). It is finished, Lonia! All that Jesus had to do to save sinners was completed. Now, God can receive sinners back to Himself, for the sake of Jesus Christ. In 1 Peter 3:15, we read, 'For Christ also hath once suffered for sins, the just for the unjust, that he might bring us to God, being put to death in the flesh, but quickened by the Spirit.'"

Lonia still had more questions. "Does God say that children can be saved?"

Grandma answered, "Of course, Lonia; there are many encouraging stories about godly children in the Bible. In the book of Mark, there is a story about mothers who brought their children to Jesus; the disciples tried to keep the children away, so they wouldn't bother Jesus. But Jesus was displeased; do you know what He said to the disciples? He rebuked them, and said, 'Suffer the little children to come unto me, and forbid them not: for of such is the kingdom of heaven' (Mark 10:14). Do you know what Jesus did when the children came to Him? The Bible says, 'And he took them up in his arms, put his hands upon them and blessed them' (Mark 10:16). Lonia, Jesus is able, ready, and willing to save little children! Never think you are too young to come to Jesus."

Lonia was encouraged and excited about this good news, but she just had to be sure of what she was hearing. "Grandma," she asked once again, "what must I do for Jesus to save and bless me?"

"The Philippian jailor asked Paul the exact same question, and so I will give you Paul's answer: 'Believe on the Lord Jesus Christ, and thou shalt be saved' (Acts 16:31)."

"But Grandma, am I just to believe with my mind that Jesus will save me? Should I just say right now that I believe, and then I will be saved?"

"No, my dear. Too many people think that just saying the words, 'I believe in Jesus,' will save them. It takes much more than just saying the words with your mouth."

"Well, what else does it take?" Lonia asked.

"You have to believe with your whole heart!" answered Grandma Kaplan (Rom. 10:9). "God puts a need for salvation in your heart, and you beg the Lord for forgiveness and mercy. By grace, you believe in the forgiving power of Jesus' blood, and the Lord saves you, just like the prayer in Jeremiah that says, 'Heal me, O LORD, and I shall be healed; save me, and I shall be saved' (Jer. 17:14). When we call upon the Lord with our hearts, we know that God hears us, and will save us; God promises us this when He says, 'For whosoever shall call upon the name of the Lord shall be saved' (Rom. 10:13)."

Dear friends, when God teaches us that we are lost, He also teaches us how to be saved. Have you believed on the Lord Jesus Christ with your whole heart? Have you been washed in the blood of Jesus Christ?

Chapter 24

Joy and Sorrow

Lonia spent the entire afternoon with Grandma. Grandma loved speaking of the Lord. Lonia was so thankful to have such a dear friend, especially one who knew the Lord so well. Later that evening, Lonia was eating her dinner, when she heard a knock on the door; she looked up to see Mary, her nurse, standing in the doorway with a smile on her face.

"May I come in? I have good news," said Mary.

"Of course, Mary," Lonia answered. "I'd love to hear your good news!"

"Well," Mary continued, "remember how you wished to go back to the Harmsons? Guess what? The doctor has given you permission to leave the hospital! He is very happy with your progress, and thinks that it will do you good to be outside in the fresh air, among your friends again. What do you think of that?"

Mary looked eagerly at Lonia, but did not see the

enthusiastic response she had expected. Instead, Lonia's face clouded over.

"But, Mary," Lonia answered, "what about Grandma? I love her so much! I can't leave her here in the hospital alone. Besides, who will I talk to about the Lord?"

"Lonia, you can't stay here forever. I'm sure you'll be able to visit Mrs. Kaplan whenever you'd like. Besides, you'll have Uncle Hank, Priscilla, and the Harmsons to talk to about Jesus," replied Mary kindly.

"I suppose you're right, Mary," sighed Lonia. "I shall miss Grandma, but it *would* be wonderful to be with the Harmsons again. When must I leave?"

"Tomorrow morning," answered Mary, and she kissed Lonia on the forehead. "Now get some rest, Lonia. Tomorrow will be a big day." She left the room quietly and closed the door.

Lonia looked down at the bustling street. Tomorrow she'd be leaving on that very street—leaving Grandma forever. Her mind returned to the many conversations they'd had together, and how they had cried and laughed together over the past few weeks. Grandma had become a very special part of Lonia's life; she had made the Lord so real to Lonia, and explained so beautifully how God saves sinners. Lonia smiled as she remembered one afternoon, when she had gone to Grandma's room in deep distress, fearing that God would never save her. Grandma had comforted her with words from John that said, "All that the Father giveth me shall come to me; and him that cometh to me, I will in no wise cast out. If any man thirst, let him come unto me and drink. He that believeth on me, as the scripture hath said, out of his belly shall flow rivers of living water" (John 6:37, 8:37-38). Greatly consoled by these words of hope through the power of the Holy Spirit, she believed in Christ alone for her salvation. She believed with her whole heart that Jesus welcomed her into His arms. She no longer feared that Jesus would reject her. She believed that Jesus had brought every one of her sins to the cross on Calvary, and had paid for them with His own precious blood. He had given her His very own righteousness! She was amazed that Jesus loved her so much that He would be willing to give His own life for her. What joy Lonia experienced that day; how she cried and thanked the Lord! She was forgiven! She was made righteous before God through the perfect righteousness of Jesus Christ.

As Lonia thought back on all that had happened to her over the past few months, she knew that God had been in control all along. Even the accident was a part of God's plan to bring her to the hospital, to bring Grandma into her life, and to eventually bring her to salvation.

Lonia decided to say goodnight to Grandma before climbing into bed. Holding onto the wall for support, she made her way slowly down the hall towards Grandma's room; Lonia smiled as she heard Grandma's sweet voice singing. She sang loudly and clearly, and Lonia listened carefully to make out the words.

> *When I in righteousness at last*
> *Thy glorious face shall see,*
> *When all the weary night is past,*

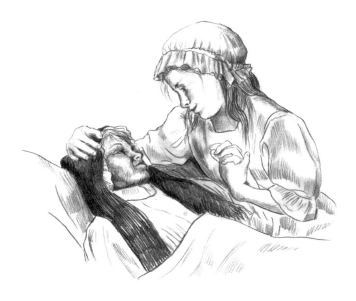

"Grandma?" she asked anxiously. "Are you alright?"

> *And I awake with Thee*
> *To view the glories that abide,*
> *Then, then I shall be satisfied!*
> — Psalter 31:7

Lonia arrived at Grandma's room to find her lying in her bed, her eyes turned upward, and her face beaming with joy. Lonia approached her bed.

"Grandma?" she asked anxiously. "Are you alright?"

Grandma turned her head slowly and smiled. "Oh, Lonia, He says to me, 'Fear not, for it is your Father's good pleasure to give you the kingdom'" (Luke 12:32).

"She's talking about dying!" Lonia thought frantically. Sobbing, she cried, "Grandma, don't leave me!"

But Grandma closed her eyes. She smiled peacefully, and whispered, "Even so, come, Lord Jesus."

Dear friends, Lonia was saved! She went to Jesus for forgiveness, believed on Him, and was forgiven. Grandma was washed in the blood of the Lamb, and she was ready to meet the Lord. If heaven would be yours at death, Christ must be yours in life. Is He? Are you forgiven, ready to meet your Maker?

Chapter 25

Not Forsaken

Lonia was terrified; she had never seen anyone die before. As quickly as her weak legs would allow, she rushed to call the doctors. But by the time they arrived, Grandma had already died, her face beaming. Lonia was greatly troubled. Grandma was gone forever! Lonia knew that she was forever with the Lord, but she ached at the thought of never seeing Grandma again. Feeling scared and abandoned, she cried out, "Lord, help me! I cannot bear this burden alone!"

The Lord heard her cry, and calmed Lonia, gently reminding her, "Lo, I am with you alway, even unto the end of the world" (Matt. 28:20). In the midst of all the commotion, Mary consoled Lonia, and helped her to her room. Lonia's sobs were heart-breaking; Mary could see that she was greatly pained. "Dear Lord," prayed Mary, "comfort her with Thy Word." Mary brought Lonia to her chair, and sat down beside her.

"Lonia," she said gently, "listen to what God says to you in this moment of fear and grief." Mary read from Isaiah 41 these words: "Fear thou not; for I am with thee: be not dismayed; for I am thy God: I will strengthen thee; yea, I will help thee; yea, I will uphold thee with the right hand of my righteousness."

As Mary read, Lonia's sobs quieted, and a sense of peace filled her heart. She felt the comforting arms of God around her, calming her and giving her strength.

The hours passed. Lonia spent much time in prayer that night. Finally, the morning light began to shine through the hospital window. "Today I leave the hospital," Lonia thought. Slowly, she got up from her bed, washed, and began to prepare her few belongings to go. She decided to take a walk down the hall to see Grandma's room one last time. As she peered into the room, an eerie feeling filled her heart. The bed was made with fresh sheets, and the room was clean, ready for its next occupant. Tears filled her eyes as she looked at the empty room. "Oh, Father," she prayed. "I am ready to leave now. I never thought my life would change this quickly! Nevertheless, not my will, but Thy will be done. Lord, help me as I leave this place."

As she whispered these words, she felt a hand on her shoulder; she turned around to find Uncle Hank standing behind her. "Are you alright, Lonia?" he asked with compassion.

"Yes," answered Lonia cautiously. "Uncle Hank, Grandma died last night. Now she is with the Lord forever."

"Lonia, did you ever read in the Bible that 'there is a friend that sticketh closer than a brother' (Prov. 18:24)"?

"Oh, Uncle Hank, it is true. Jesus is closer to me than any earthly friend, even Grandma," sighed Lonia.

Uncle Hank nodded, and said, "Jesus knows all our sorrows, because He Himself is a 'man of sorrows, and acquainted with grief' (Isa. 53:3). He says to His children, 'I will never leave thee nor forsake thee' (Heb. 13:5). He knows your grief, Lonia, and He is always with you. Through this difficult time, God is teaching you a lesson about how precious Jesus is! Through these trials, you will discover that God is all-knowing, all-sufficient, and always faithful. He uses these trials to bring you closer and closer to Himself."

"Yes, Uncle Hank, I know it's true. Even last night, Mary read God's words to me when I was sad, and the Lord sent me comfort and strength. He is so good to me!"

Dear friend, Jesus will never forsake you in life, in troubles, or in death. Is He your Friend? Are you living out of Him?

Chapter 26

Departing

The hour had finally arrived for Lonia to leave the hospital. Uncle Hank carried all her belongings and Priscilla walked by her side, giving her support. Lonia was thankful for the presence of her dear friends, but the pang of Grandma's death was still sharp. She made her way down the hallway and finally arrived at the doorway. As she stepped out to the waiting carriage, she froze with fear. She stared at the two large horses pulling the carriage; memories of the accident flashed through her mind, and she stepped back in fear.

"Uncle Hank," she whispered, "do we have to take the carriage home? Isn't there a safer way?"

"Lonia, the horses are well-trained. They will not hurt you, I promise. You needn't be afraid," he replied, and put his strong arm around her. "Do you remember how God shut the mouths of the lions when Daniel was in their den? Lonia, trust God! He is in control of all things, even these horses. He will take care of you."

Lonia was somewhat relieved; cautiously, she stepped closer to the carriage and climbed in. The ride home was fine, and Lonia was thankful to see that God had heard her prayer and protected them. As they pulled past the great iron gate of the Harmson home, Lonia's heart was filled with joy. How glad she was to have such a wonderful family to come home to! Her memories of being an orphan and a servant girl flashed through her mind, and she rejoiced at how different her life had become with Uncle Hank and the Harmson family. God had given her so much. She thought back to the hospital, and how she had longed to be back with this family; God had answered that prayer, too.

The weeks passed quickly at the Harmson home. During the days, she and Priscilla talked for hours; at night, they joined in family worship and singing around the fireplace.

After three beautiful weeks, Lonia was strong enough to leave the Harmsons, and Uncle Hank returned to take Lonia to her new home. Uncle Hank and Lonia were thankful to hear that the Harmsons had made all the necessary arrangements for the long, difficult trip home. The day of Lonia's departure arrived, and she awoke with a lump in her throat. It was going to be difficult to leave such wonderful friends. That morning they all ate breakfast together and spoke of the faithfulness of the Lord; they smiled, thinking of how blessed they were that the Lord had brought them together. After breakfast, Mr.

Harmson read about the promise of God's protection from Psalm 91: "He shall give his angels charge over thee, to keep thee in all thy ways" (v. 11). They prayed together, thanking God for His blessings, and pleading for God's protection in the future.

Uncle Hank put the bags in the carriage, and made all the necessary preparations for leaving. Lonia and Priscilla walked out into the fields for some time alone. They walked arm in arm and chatted together about the times they had shared. Before long, Uncle Hank was ready to go, and he and the Harmsons walked out to get the girls. The precious scene they found would forever be etched upon their hearts.

Lonia and Priscilla were sitting in the grassy field behind the barn; their hands were clasped together, and their heads were bowed.

Lonia and Priscilla were sitting in the grassy field behind the barn; their hands were clasped together, and their heads were bowed. Priscilla was praying. As they heard the depth of their prayers, and the tenderness of their expression, Uncle Hank and the Harmsons had no doubt that these were godly, blessed girls. Uncle Hank and the Harmsons listened with joy, and smiled at these two godly girls having sweet communion with their heavenly Father. Never had they heard such God-glorifying prayers, pleadings, and praise from children. Drawing closer, they could make out the words of Lonia's beautiful prayer:

Dear Lord, Thy ways are wonderful; Thy grace is amazing. Thy love is beyond anything I could have imagined or deserved. Never would I have sought Thee, if Thou hadst not sought me first. Never would I have cried for mercy, if Thou hadst not taught me my sinfulness. But through Jesus, Thou hast looked upon me and washed all my sins away. It is His death and blood that has made me clean. It is His righteousness that has clothed me. Please, Lord, lead Priscilla and me in the paths of righteousness, for Jesus' sake. Give us more love for Thee, and more hatred for sin. May Thy Word be our guide. May goodness and mercy follow us all the days of our lives. And though we may never see each other again, when death comes and the Judgment Day arrives, wilt Thou say to us, "Come ye blessed of my Father, inherit the kingdom prepared for you from the foundation of the world." Lord, may that day come soon, when we can sing in heaven, "Worthy is the Lamb that was slain to receive power and riches and wisdom, and strength, and honor and glory and blessing." For the sake of Jesus Christ. Amen.

Priscilla and Lonia hugged each other tightly. Tears flowed down their faces; their hearts were full of joy and sorrow.

"Priscilla," said Lonia sincerely, "thank you for your love, your care, and your prayers. Remember, we shall meet again in heaven, and be forever with all those who love the Lord Jesus Christ in sincerity and truth."

The goodbye was bittersweet; the Harmson family waved until the carriage disappeared around the corner. As they turned to walk back home, they wept; the love they felt for their friends was great, because they shared the love of God in their hearts.

Dear friend, the parting of these friends was difficult, but they would surely meet again in heaven. They were washed in the blood of the Lamb. Are you? Lonia was a child of the Lord. Do not rest until you too are a son or daughter of God. Repent and believe the gospel. As there was room in Christ for Lonia, so there is room for you!